# Emily Dickinson

by Maurene Hinds

**Content Consultant**
Martha Nell Smith
Professor of English
University of Maryland

CORE
LIBRARY

Published by ABDO Publishing Company, PO Box 398166, Minneapolis, MN 55439. Copyright © 2013 by Abdo Consulting Group, Inc. International copyrights reserved in all countries. No part of this book may be reproduced in any form without written permission from the publisher. The Core Library™ is a trademark and logo of ABDO Publishing Company.

Printed in the United States of America,
North Mankato, Minnesota
112012
012013

Editor: Kari Cornell
Series Designer: Becky Daum

Cataloging-in-Publication Data
Hinds, Maurene.
  Emily Dickinson / Maurene Hinds.
    p. cm. -- (Great American authors)
Includes bibliographical references and index.
ISBN 978-1-61783-716-6
1. Dickinson, Emily, 1830-1886--Juvenile literature.  2. Poets, American--19th century--Biography--Juvenile literature.   I. Title.
811/.4--dc23
[B]
                                        2012946800

Photo Credits: Hulton Archive/Getty Images, cover, 1, 30; Dennis Vandal/AP Images, 4, 22, 45; Library of Congress, 7; Lebrecht Music and Arts Photo Library/Alamy, 9; Amherst College Archives and Special Collections/Emily Dickinson Museum/AP Images, 10, 18; Bettmann/Corbis/AP Images, 13, 20, 32, 34; Red Line Editorial, 15, 35; Carol Lollis/The Daily Hampshire Gazette/AP Images, 16; William S. Warren (Boston)/Picture History, 26, 28; Beth Harpaz/AP Images, 38

# CONTENTS

# CHAPTER ONE

# A Quiet Life

In the mid-to late 1800s, a mysterious woman lived in her parents' two-story home in Amherst, Massachusetts. Many people in the small town had heard of her. Few had seen her. She left the house only when she chose to and welcomed only certain visitors. When she did have visitors, she sometimes spoke to them from behind a curtain or from another room. The woman never married. She spent much of

The Homestead, where Emily Dickinson was born and lived for most of her life, is still located on Main Street in Amherst, Massachusetts.

her time in her upstairs room, often looking out over the family garden.

This woman was Emily Dickinson. Few of those living in Amherst knew it at the time, but Dickinson spent her days writing poetry. By 1865 she had written more than 1,000 poems. Dickinson carefully copied 800 of these poems into small books that she sewed together herself. These small books were called fascicles. Dickinson shared these books with very few people. Instead she hid them, and they were discovered after her death. She also wrote hundreds of letters to friends and family during her lifetime. Although much of Dickinson's life remains a mystery, what

## Woman in White

Dickinson is said to have worn an unusual style of clothing. Beginning around her late 20s, she was often seen in her garden wearing white or mostly white. This helped keep her life simple, so she could focus on her writings. The clothing was easy to clean with bleach, and everything always matched.

This print of a young Emily Dickinson appeared on the first pages of *The Letters of Emily Dickinson*, published in 1894.

we do know of her life has been pieced together from her letters.

## Early Childhood Years

Emily Elizabeth Dickinson was born on December 10, 1830, in Amherst, Massachusetts, a small town approximately 94 miles (151 km) from Boston. Her childhood was quite ordinary. Her family, in some ways, was not. Emily's father, Edward Dickinson, was strict. The Dickinsons were known well in Amherst, and Edward worked very hard to succeed. He was one of the town's first lawyers. He was also treasurer for Amherst College, as his father was before him. Later in life he served as a congressman. Emily's mother, Emily Norcross Dickinson, stayed at home with the children, as many mothers did at the time. But she may have suffered from depression, so she sometimes spent time in her room, away from her children.

Emily was the second of three children. She was very close to her older brother, William Austin, known as Austin. They shared a love of reading. Emily was also close to her younger sister, Lavinia, whom she

Emily Dickinson, *left*, with brother Austin, *center*, and sister Vinnie, *right*, in 1840

called "Vinnie." Their father often worked away from home and their mother was often ill. The Dickinson children spent a lot of time together. They became good friends.

## School Years

Emily started school at Amherst Academy when she was ten years old. She made many lasting friendships there. Similar to other young girls, she was fond of some of her teachers. She and her friends talked about the boys they liked. Emily had a happy and social school life.

# CHAPTER TWO

# Beginning to Write

In 1847 when Emily was 16, she left for Mount Holyoke Female Seminary, a boarding school several miles from Amherst. This was the first time she had spent any time away from home. It wasn't easy. In the mid-1800s, religion was studied in school and at home. At Mount Holyoke, students were expected to announce their devotion to God in front of everyone. Emily was unable to do this.

Dickinson at Mount Holyoke Female Seminary in late 1847 or early 1848

She had always struggled with whether or not she believed in God. She decided to leave Mount Holyoke and move back to Amherst in August 1848. The religious focus at the school may have been one of the reasons she left. Her parents also worried about her health because she suffered from severe colds.

## Returning to Amherst

When Emily returned home from Mount Holyoke, she enjoyed the life of a normal teenager in the mid-1800s. She attended parties, went on carriage rides, and had daily visitors.

After only one year, Emily decided to leave Mount Holyoke Female Seminary and move back to Amherst.

She also spent time with many friends from her days at Amherst Academy.

Emily took a serious interest in writing poetry in her late teens and early 20s. She had always been a letter writer and had crafted some poems as a child. But now Emily started writing more poetry. Her brother, Austin, was writing poems as well. Their father was typical of fathers at the time in many ways. He expected different things from his son than he did from his daughters. He liked the idea of a son who wrote. When Austin shared his writing, his father seemed to enjoy it. Emily, on the other hand, hid most of her poems from her family and friends. Perhaps she didn't want to share her work, or maybe she thought her father would disapprove.

## Young Adulthood

In 1849 when Dickinson was 19, her father bought her a puppy. She named the dog Carlo. Carlo was a Newfoundland, a very large breed of dog that was popular at the time. Emily's sister was away at school, her father was away on business, and her mother was ill. Carlo was a companion and friend to Dickinson. She mentioned Carlo in some of her poems as well as her letters. Together they took long walks, during which Dickinson's imagination could run free.

Around this same time, Dickinson met Susan Gilbert, and the two became quite close. Both women were intelligent, and both loved to read. Susan and Emily enjoyed talking about ideas. Emily's brother also had an interest in Susan. When Austin proposed to Susan in 1853, Emily began to feel left out. In Emily's

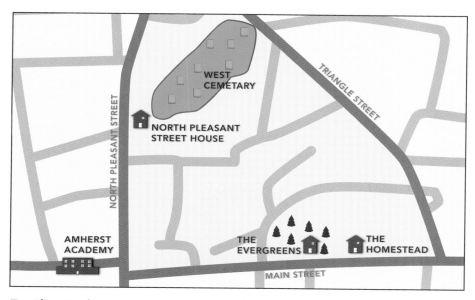

**Emily Dickinson's Amherst, 1886**

**The Homestead:** Built by Samuel Fowler Dickinson in 1813, this was the house where Emily was born in 1830, where she returned to live with her family in 1855, and where she died in 1886.

**North Pleasant Street House:** The Dickinson family lived in this house from 1840 until 1855.

**Amherst Academy:** Emily attended school here from 1840 until 1847.

**The Evergreens:** Edward Dickinson built this house in 1856 for William Austin Dickinson and his new bride, Susan Harrington Gilbert. It was located next door to The Homestead.

**West Cemetery:** Emily was buried here in the Dickinson family plot in 1886.

view, she was losing her brother and a friend to marriage. Emily, her brother, and Susan still remained close.

The Dickinson's beloved Homestead was originally built in 1813 for Emily's grandparents.

## The Homestead

In 1855 when Dickinson was 25, the family moved to the house where her grandparents had lived before leaving Amherst. Edward Dickinson spent a lot of money fixing up the house, which was called The Homestead. He added a conservatory, a room with many glass windows, where flowers could grow year-round. Emily enjoyed gardening, something her mother had taught her and Vinnie to do. Vinnie and Emily, both unmarried, each had her own room.

Emily's room was upstairs where she could look out over the garden.

After the move, Emily did not go out as much as she used to. Part of the reason for this change may have been her mother's health. Her mother was not well before the move. After they settled into The Homestead, she became an invalid. She stayed in bed and needed constant care. Emily and Vinnie took care of their mother for many years.

## A Brother's Marriage

Austin and Susan married at Susan's aunt's home in Geneva, New York, in 1856. The Dickinson family did not attend the wedding. Emily's mother's poor health made travel impossible. But Austin and Susan soon moved next door to The Homestead. Edward Dickinson had built a new home for the couple. They called it The Evergreens.

Austin and Susan often had parties. Many people visited, including well-known writers of the time. It is not known whether Emily met these writers, but

At 29 years old, Emily Dickinson, *left*, poses for a photo with friend Kate Scott Turner in 1859.

she would sometimes play the piano for Austin and Susan's guests.

Austin and Susan were married during a time when Emily lost many friends. Some married and moved away. Others became ill with tuberculosis or scarlet fever, two serious illnesses that struck many. Between 1851 and 1854, at least 30 of Emily's friends died. Some she had known since childhood.

Even though Emily experienced grief and loss, she also found joy. Austin and Susan had three children. Edward (Ned) was born in 1861, Martha was born in 1866, and Thomas Gilbert (Gib) was born in 1875. Emily enjoyed spending time with the family.

## Emily Chooses Not to Marry

Before long Dickinson reached the age when most women did not marry if they were not already wed. In the late 1800s, a woman who did not marry by her mid-to late 20s was considered too old for marriage. While some of her letters and poems suggest she may have loved a few of the men in her life, and male friends came to visit, she never married. This is not what was expected of women in her time. But Dickinson's father seemed to support her interests.

### Emily's Private World

Many stories make it seem as if Emily had few friends. But in her youth, Emily enjoyed a busy social life. She was also friends with men. It's likely that some of those men were in love with her. Emily may have had feelings for one of her married friends, Samuel Bowles. It may also be that she had a marriage proposal from a man named George Gould, who graduated from Amherst College.

# CHAPTER THREE

# A Prolific Writer

By her 20s, Dickinson was writing seriously. She shared hundreds of her poems with her sister-in-law, Susan. Dickinson often included poems with gifts she gave to friends and family. But she kept her writing secret from many people. There were many poems she kept hidden in a drawer. She wrote the poems, sewed the pages together to create small books, and tucked the books away.

Dickinson wrote most of her poems at this small writing desk in her room at home in Amherst. From her bedroom windows, Dickinson could look out over the family gardens.

While doing her chores, Dickinson would often jot down notes to use later. She sewed pockets into her dresses to keep a pencil and paper. When not taking care of her mother or doing housework, Dickinson enjoyed spending time in the garden. There she often took time to listen to the birds, watch a butterfly flutter past, or wait to see a bee pollinate a flower.

## A Love of Nature

While a number of Dickinson's poems were sad or dealt with loss, others were lively and upbeat. Many of her poems show a sense of hope. One of her most beloved poems, titled "Hope," describes hope as "the thing with feathers." She enjoyed nature and often wrote about the outdoors in her poems.

Dickinson also had a vivid imagination. She loved to read literature and mythology and would sometimes use mythology in her poems. Dickinson's imagination allowed her to visit places she had never seen in person. In one well-known poem, "I Never Saw a Moor," she describes seeing the ocean, which she had never visited.

## An Unusual Style

One of Dickinson's most well-known poems tells readers to tell the truth "slant." In many ways, this describes Dickinson's approach to writing. The idea of telling something "slant" means to write about it in a new way with an unexpected turn. In some of her work, Dickinson addresses an idea but does not explain what it means, leaving the reader to figure it out. Her poems also have both unclear ideas followed by very clear ideas, which can be confusing. This paradox, or placement of

## Breaking the Rules

Dickinson's poems were different from other poetry at the time. She did not follow the rules of writing, such as punctuation, spelling, or capitalization. She used dashes and capitalization to draw attention to ideas or words. She would use slant rhymes, words that nearly rhymed, but not exactly. Writer and literary critic Thomas Wentworth Higginson suggested Dickinson fix her poems to follow the rules. But she ignored his advice and continued to write in her own style.

Thomas Wentworth Higginson wrote many letters to Dickinson during her lifetime. He reviewed the poems she sent and offered ideas on her work.

opposing ideas together, is a central theme in much of Dickinson's work. Dickinson looked at the world through fresh eyes, and she crafted highly original poems.

For Dickinson, good poetry affected the reader physically. She once wrote about the effects of poetry. "If I read a book and it makes my body so cold no fire can ever warm me I know *that* is poetry. If I feel physically as if the top of my head were taken off, I know *that* is poetry. These are the ways I know it. Is there any other way?" Susan Dickinson said something very similar when she wrote in response to Emily's poem, "Safe in Their Alabaster Chambers," "I always go to the fire and get warm after thinking of it, but I *never* can again."

## Literary Friendships

In 1862 when Dickinson was in her early 30s, she sent four poems to Thomas Wentworth Higginson. Higginson had published "Letter to a Young Contributor" in the *Atlantic Monthly*. In the essay, Higginson encouraged young writers. Higginson did send a reply to Dickinson. He decided not to publish her poems then, but the two began to write letters back and forth about her work. She wrote him more than 60 letters and sent him almost 100 poems.

There were others who supported Dickinson in her writing. Susan, who read Dickinson's poems from

Writer Helen Hunt Jackson became friends with Dickinson when they were classmates at Amherst Academy.

the time they were teenagers until Dickinson died in 1913, provided the most encouragement. Dickinson's childhood friend, Helen Hunt Jackson, also urged her to write. Jackson became a famous author for her work, *Ramona*. Ben Newton, who worked with Dickinson's father, became a good friend to her and helped guide her reading. He often suggested books for her to read, including Ralph Waldo Emerson's work called *Poems*. Samuel Bowles, a family friend and editor of the *Republican*, also provided feedback on her writing. Dickinson and Bowles wrote letters to each other for many years. At least ten of Dickinson's poems were published in the *Republican* and other newspapers and journals including the *Drum Beat*, the *Brooklyn Daily Union*, and *Round Table*.

## Published

Only ten of Dickinson's poems were published in newspapers or magazines during her lifetime. These poems were published anonymously, without an author's name. One kind of publication, called "coterie" publication, is to send poems with letters or hand them to friends. Dickinson sent out hundreds and hundreds of her poems in letters.

In this photo taken in 1850, Dickinson is around 20 years old.

The following is one of Dickinson's well-known poems. It is short but has deep meaning. As you read, see if you can figure out what she is trying to say:

*A word is dead*

*When it is said,*

*Some say.*

*I say it just*

*Begins to live*

*That day.*

Source: Emily Dickinson. Poems by Emily Dickinson, Third Series. *Boston: Roberts Brothers, 1896. Print. 18.*

## What's the Big Idea?

Take a closer look at Dickinson's poem. What is the main idea? Why would someone say a word is "dead" when it is spoken? What does the poem say about words instead? What lines or words from the poem show the poet's meaning? How is the poem commenting on readers?

# CHAPTER FOUR

# The Later Years

B y the mid-1860s, Dickinson was dealing with ongoing eye problems. She went to Boston in April 1864 to get treatment. While she was there she stayed with her cousins. She received more eye treatments from April to October 1865. The problem seemed to have improved.

Carlo, Dickinson's beloved dog, died in 1866. She mentioned the death in a brief letter to Higginson.

Few photos were taken of Dickinson as she grew older and kept to herself. This portrait of the poet was completed during her younger years.

This miniature painting of a young Dickinson is part of the Dickinson family collection.

It is her only direct mention of Carlo's death. With the letter, she included a poem titled "My Cricket." She rarely gave her poems titles, and the poem is now known by the first line, "Further in Summer / than the Birds." For Dickinson, Carlo had been as dependable as the chirping of crickets on a summer evening. After he was gone, she felt lost.

In 1882 Austin began an affair with a married woman, Mabel Loomis Todd. The affair lasted

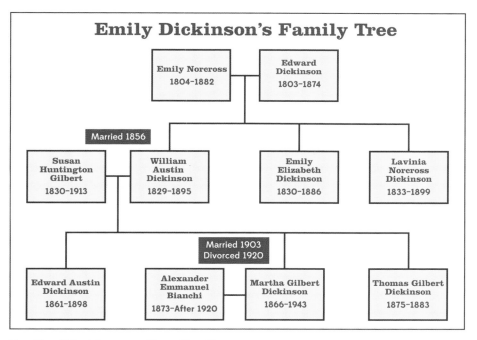

**Emily Dickinson Family Tree**

The Dickinson family was known well throughout Amherst. Study the family tree. What do you learn about Dickinson's family that you didn't know from reading the text?

13 years. Emily and Austin did not remain as close as they once had. Emily and Susan remained friends.

## Grief and Loss

In the last 20 years of her life, Dickinson did not write in the same ways she had as a younger woman. Her father died suddenly in Boston in 1874 after he collapsed while giving a speech in the state legislature. Dickinson spent most of these years caring for her mother who remained ill and bedridden until her death in 1882. Caring for her mother took a toll on Dickinson's health as well.

In 1883 her nephew Gib died from typhoid fever. After his death, Dickinson became even more private. She rarely left the house. When visitors came, she did not speak to some of them face-to-face. Dickinson became ill soon after Gib died. Dickinson died on May 15, 1886. The official cause of death was Bright's disease, a disease that affects the kidneys.

## What She Left Behind

After Dickinson died, Vinnie destroyed her sister's letters, which was the custom at the time. But while she was searching through Emily's things, Vinnie discovered 40 small handmade books filled with her sister's poems. Vinnie wanted Emily's work to be read and appreciated, but to read through it all would take a long time. There were almost 1,800 poems, and Dickinson's handwriting is known to be hard to read.

Susan Dickinson, to whom Emily had sent more poems than any other person, started to work on the poems. Within a few months, Susan sent some of Emily's poems to *The Century* for publication. She asked Higginson to publish a book of Emily's poetry paired with illustrations and short writings to Austin and Susan's children. Higginson was not convinced the book Susan suggested would be popular with readers. After a while, Vinnie became impatient with Susan's progress. Susan was grieving the loss of her best friend Emily, her youngest son Gib, and one of her sisters, so she worked slowly. Mabel Loomis Todd agreed to help. Mabel went through the poems, and Vinnie contacted Higginson once again. Higginson finally said he would

## A Fan of Brontë

Thomas Wentworth Higginson spoke at Dickinson's funeral. He read a poem of Dickinson's choice, "No Coward Soul," by Brontë. Brontë was one of Dickinson's favorite poets. Brontë experimented with form and punctuation as well, although not to the extent Dickinson did.

Dickinson is buried in West Cemetery in Amherst. Her original gravestone was simply marked with her initials, but her niece, Martha Dickinson Bianchi, eventually replaced it with this stone.

help publish the poems. In the end, Vinnie paid for the costs of publication.

## Dickinson's Poems in Print

While preparing Dickinson's poems for publication, both Higginson and Mabel made changes to the poems to correct the grammar and punctuation. *Poems by Emily Dickinson* was published in three volumes in 1890, 1891, and 1896. Mabel also found and put together some of what remained of Dickinson's letters. *Letters of Emily Dickinson*, which did not include many of Dickinson's most important letters, was published as two volumes in 1894.

Eventually Dickinson's niece, Martha Dickinson Bianchi, went through the poems. In her volumes, Bianchi included many poems and letters from Emily to Susan that Mabel had left out. She also included many more details about Dickinson's life and writing habits than Mabel had been able to give. In 1955 *The Poems of Emily Dickinson* was published and edited by Thomas H. Johnson. The original poems Dickinson had placed in handmade books were published in 1981. This edition featured photographs of

## A Lifetime of Letters

Letter writing was the main form of communication in the 1800s. Dickinson wrote many letters, both as a child and as an adult. While some people say she lived without much contact with others, she never stopped writing letters. Most of Dickinson's letters were burned after she died, as was the custom. Much of what is known about her comes from the letters that were not destroyed.

the manuscripts after they were assembled by Ralph Franklin.

Dickinson's poems appeal to readers of all ages. Some poems are short, playful, and often read in elementary schools. Other poems are complicated and are studied in college. Dickinson inspired poets in the early 1900s to play with form and style in their writing. Today Dickinson is considered one of America's best poets.

## FURTHER EVIDENCE

There is quite a bit of information about Dickinson's published works in Chapter Four. If you could pick out the main point of the chapter, what would it be? What evidence was given to support that point? Visit the Web site below to learn more about the publication of Dickinson's poems after her death. Choose a quote from the Web site and write a few sentences explaining how the quote you found relates to this chapter.

### Emily Dickinson Museum: The Posthumous Discovery of Dickinson's Poems

www.emilydickinsonmuseum.org/posthumous_publication

Most of Dickinson's poems were not printed in magazines or books while she was still alive, but that did not stop her from writing. And she did not change her writing style to please others. The following poem describes how she felt about the success of her work:

*I'm Nobody! Who are you?*

*Are you—Nobody—Too?*

*Then there's a pair of us!*

*Don't tell! they'd advertise—you know!*


*How dreary—to be—Somebody!*

*How public—like a Frog—*

*To tell one's name—the livelong June—*

*To an admiring Bog!*

*Source: Emily Dickinson.* Poems, Second Series. *Boston: Roberts Brothers, 1891. Print. 21.*

## What's the Big Idea?

Take a close look at this poem. What is Dickinson trying to say about being somebody? Pick out two details she uses to make her point. What do you notice about the way she uses the word "nobody"?

# IMPORTANT DATES

**1830**
Emily Elizabeth Dickinson is born in Amherst, Massachusetts, on December 10.

**1847**
Dickinson begins school at Mount Holyoke Female Seminary.

**1849**
Dickinson's father, Edward, buys her a dog, Carlo.

**1855**
The Dickinson family moves to The Homestead in November. Emily and her sister, Vinnie, take over care of their mother.

**1856**
Austin Dickinson and Susan Gilbert marry.

**1862**
Dickinson begins correspondence with Thomas Wentworth Higginson.

**1866**
Carlo dies in January.

**1874**
Dickinson's father dies.

**1882**
Dickinson's mother, Emily Norcross Dickinson, dies.

**1886**
Dickinson dies on May 15 at the age of 55.

**1890**
Dickinson's first set of poems is published.

# KEY WORKS

## Letters of Emily Dickinson

A more complete collection of Dickinson's letters to friends and family than the book of letters edited by Mabel Loomis Todd. This book includes many letters to Susan Dickinson that were not printed in the earlier book.

Dickinson, Emily. *Letters of Emily Dickinson.* Eds. Thomas H. Johnson and Theodora Ward. Cambridge, MA: Belknap, 1958.

## Poems

This was the first volume of poems edited by Todd and Higginson. The poems were edited for punctuation, grammar, and sometimes rhyme scheme. When the first volume of poems was well received, second and third collections were published.

Dickinson, Emily. *Poems.* Eds. Thomas Wentworth Higgins and Mabel Loomis Todd. Boston: Roberts Brothers, 1890.

## The Poems of Emily Dickinson

This well-known volume contains all of Dickinson's work and was compiled by Thomas H. Johnson, a literary scholar. He used Dickinson's original works in the compilation, presenting the poems closer to how Dickinson wrote them. He also published the poems in the order in which they were written.

Dickinson, Emily. *The Poems of Emily Dickinson.* Ed. Thomas H. Johnson. Cambridge, MA: Belknap, 1955.

## The Single Hound: Poems of a Lifetime

This collection of poems includes an introduction by Dickinson's niece, Martha Dickinson Bianchi, who edited the book.

Dickinson, Emily. *The Single Hound: Poems of a Lifetime.* Ed. Martha Dickinson Bianchi. Boston: Little, Brown, and Company, 1914.

## Take a Stand

Chapter Three discusses the way Dickinson broke many rules of writing and grammar in her poetry. Thomas Wentworth Higginson wanted to correct her errors, but Dickinson refused. If you were Dickinson, would you have made the changes Higginson suggested? Write a short essay explaining your opinion. Include reasons for your opinion, and give some facts and details to support those reasons.

## Tell the Tale

This book covers important relationships in Dickinson's life, such as the one with her dog, Carlo. Which relationships are important to you? Write 200 words that tell the true story of a friendship or important relationship in your life. Be sure to set the scene, develop a sequence of events, and write a conclusion.

## Why Do I Care?

Because Dickinson did not travel much, she used her imagination when she wrote. She was inspired by the books she read. What inspires you? Write a short story or poem about something you've always wanted to do or see.

## Another View

Much of Dickinson's life remains a mystery. Ask a librarian to help you find another source about Emily Dickinson. What does that source say about her life? Write a short essay comparing and contrasting the way Dickinson is portrayed.

# GLOSSARY

**bankrupt**
not having any money left to pay for expenses

**bog**
wet, spongy ground with muddy soil

**conservatory**
a greenhouse

**coterie**
to publish by sending a piece of writing in a letter or by giving it to friends

**depression**
feelings of great sadness

**invalid**
a person too sick or weak to take care of him or herself

**moor**
a place or structure to secure a ship

**paradox**
a statement that is contradictory or opposing of itself

**prolific**
producing a large quantity of something

**rhyme**
when words have the same ending sounds

**slant**
to distort or change

**treasurer**
a person in charge of money for a business or organization

# LEARN MORE

## Books

Meltzer, Milton. *Emily Dickinson*. Minneapolis: Twenty-First Century Books, 2006.

Rhodes Figley, Marty. *Emily and Carlo*. Watertown, MA: Charlesbridge, 2012.

Schoonmaker Bolin, Frances, ed. *Emily Dickinson*. New York: Sterling, 2001.

## Web Links

To learn more about Emily Dickinson, visit ABDO Publishing Company online at **www.abdopublishing.com.** Web sites about Emily Dickinson are featured on our Book Links page. These links are routinely monitored and updated to provide the most current information available.

Visit **www.mycorelibrary.com** for free additional tools for teachers and students.

# INDEX

## ABOUT THE AUTHOR

Maurene Hinds is a faculty member with American Public University and an author of several nonfiction books for teens. She lives in Montana and holds an MFA in Writing for Children and Teens from Vermont College.